Arise and Go Forth in Faith: A Journal for My Journey

I0103478

Vivianne A. Griffiths

BK
ROYSTON
Publishing

BK Royston Publishing
P. O. Box 4321 | Jeffersonville, IN 47131
502-802-5385 | http://www.bkroystonpublishing.com
bkroystonpublishing@gmail.com

Cover Design: Gad Savage, Elite Covers
Photography: Marvin Young, Multimedia Specialist

ISBN-13: 978-1-955063-62-3

Printed in the United States of America

Dedication

Greetings! This journal is dedicated to you or someone you know:

- If you are a teenager.

- If you are a woman.

- If you are a man.

- If you are young or a senior.

- If you are single or married.

- And if you want to see God in your everyday life.

- Or if you want to meet with God for the very first time, since you heard how a relationship with Him can change your life.

- And if you want to move forward with gratitude and victory in the name of Jesus Christ.

Welcome and thank you for allowing me to champion your journey!

Acknowledgement

I give honor to God, the Father, Son and Holy Ghost, for never leaving me alone on my life journey. He has given me knowledge I would not have been able to obtain on my own, and opportunities I would not have been able to realize without His direction. I am forever grateful for the relationship I have with my Lord and Savior Jesus Christ, and want my work to glorify Him.

I also am grateful for my husband and adult children who have supported me in my creative efforts in writing, and those writers and poets that have been an inspiration throughout my young adult years until the present.

Also, my Pastor Dr. Walter Malone Jr. of Canaan Christian Church, who has provided spiritual food by his sermons, which has sustained me in many aspects of my life. I am grateful for them all.

Table of Contents

Introduction

In 2019, I had the privilege of going on my first missionary trip with Rev. Dawn Sanders and her team from Pioneer International. We traveled to Cape Town, South Africa and then Johannesburg, South Africa before returning to the U.S. My assignment as the only medical team member, was to launch a medical clinic for Enon Tabernacle Missionary Baptist Church - Western Cape. The church under the leadership of Pastor Jacobus Nomdoe, and his wife Co-pastor Erica Nomdoe had established a Teen Challenge program in Capetown, that provided holistic care for the young women (who were victims of drug and sex trafficking) and the young men (who had been involved in gangs). My role included administering physical assessments and basic medical care for the young people, and providing medical supplies and creating health manuals to be used in the clinic.

Our team also provided spiritual care, through prayer, Bible lessons with life applications and singing.

Prior to going to South Africa, I had prepared a page of devotions and affirmations and gave each individual woman there her own copy. Time passed and after reviewing and pondering about what the next step should be since creating the devotions, in

2021 I reached out to Dr. Julia Royston, of BK Royston Publishing and began the literary journey of using the framework of the devotions for creating this book.

I am so excited and prayerful, that this book of devotions will remind the readers of the love and plans God has for those who believe in Him and follow His word, the Holy Bible. May it lead the reader to intentionally take time to seek and follow Him.

Christian Definition of Meditation:

A form of prayer in which a structured attempt is made to become aware of and reflect upon the revelations of God. I pray that these devotionals will help you develop the mind-set that will lead to Christian meditation.

When spending time with Jesus, find a comfortable quiet location and a time free of distractions. You may be sitting or lying down or walking in a peaceful location. Closing your eyes while sitting or lying down will keep you focused on your meditation. Breathe in the breath of God slowly and deeply through your nose with belly rising, and hold it for about 5 counts, then breathe out slowly stress, and negative thoughts with your mouth open for about 5 counts. If you have your Bible ready, then focus on a scripture on which you choose to meditate.

My Spiritual Community

I need to be in the community of Jesus believing people, so I can grow as His disciple

Life is a story of where we have come from to where we are, how we got there and where we are going. My younger sister and I were raised by Christian parents. Regardless of how imperfect they were, they made sure we were introduced to Jesus and reared in the faith. My parents separated when I was about 14 years old. Later my father obtained custody of us due to my mother's mental illness. He sent my sister and me to church every Sunday. His male co-worker was the Sunday School teacher for my age group, and as a newcomer I was a shy shrinking violet, not participating as much as my classmates.

But I kept returning each Sunday, and listening to the Bible stories and how as a teen it applied to my life. As years went by, something changed: a spark on the inside (the Holy Spirit) caused me to yearn to be a permanent part of this fellowship. At age 18, I took my younger sister with me to the church's discipleship interest classes. We learned more about the Bible, the church doctrine, and what it meant to follow Christ. After completing the classes, my sister and I joined church without our father's knowledge.

You see, he sent us to church, but - he stopped going himself after he and our mother separated. He just stayed home, reading the Bible. Later he did join another church; as the Bible says, a little child will lead them. Of all the decisions I have made in my life, being in a Christian fellowship has helped me understand that this painful temporary life can be overcome by a relationship with Jesus, leading me to everlasting joy in eternal life. I thank my parents for planting the seed. Are you trying to be a Solo Saint: not belonging to a church fellowship because you feel you can serve the Lord all by yourself? Did you know you are a missing part of the body of Christ when you are not fellowshipping with other believers? Your gift is to be shared, not hidden.

2 Corinthians 5:17 says, "Therefore if any person is [ingrafted] in Christ (the Messiah) he is a new creation (a new creature altogether); the old [previous moral and spiritual condition] has passed away. Behold the fresh *and* new has come." Amplified Bible, Classic Edition (AMPC)

Hebrews 10:25 "..not forsaking our meeting together [as believers for worship and instruction], as is the habit of some, but encouraging one another; and all the more [faithfully] as you see the day [of Christ's return] approaching." Amplified Bible

My Reflections and Meditation:

_____
_____
_____
_____
_____
_____
_____
_____
_____
_____
_____
_____
_____
_____
_____
_____
_____
_____
_____
_____
_____
_____
_____
_____
_____
_____

My Reflections and Meditation:

_____

_____

_____

_____

_____

_____

_____

_____

_____

_____

_____

_____

_____

_____

_____

_____

_____

_____

_____

_____

_____

_____

_____

_____

My Reflections and Meditation:

_____
_____
_____
_____
_____
_____
_____
_____
_____
_____
_____
_____
_____
_____
_____
_____
_____
_____
_____
_____
_____
_____
_____
_____
_____
_____

Affirmation: I will pray for God to direct me to a Christian church where I can grow as Jesus' disciple and lead others to Christ. If I am already in a Bible-believing church, I will encourage my fellow Christians in the faith.

My Thoughts

I will put away negative thoughts as I praise God.

This is so hard for me, Lord. When surrounded by negative people and circumstances, I can't seem to separate myself from the situation. Those careless whispers, which can take me down a deep hole of discontentment, surround me. I may get sucked into the abyss of gossip and naysayers. Lord, I need you to regulate my mind and give me an escape route.

How many times have you felt discouraged or angry because of whom you are surrounded by? Will you have the courage to change whom you are with before they negatively change you?

Psalm 119:11–12 says, "I have thought much about your words and stored them in my heart so that they would hold me back from sin. Blessed Lord, teach me your rules." The Living Bible (TLB)

2 Corinthians 10:5 says, "We demolish arguments and every pretension that sets itself up against the knowledge of God, and we take captive every thought to make it obedient to Christ." New International Version (NIV)

My Reflections and Meditation:

_____

_____

_____

_____

_____

_____

_____

_____

_____

_____

_____

_____

_____

_____

_____

_____

_____

_____

_____

_____

_____

_____

_____

_____

My Reflections and Meditation:

Affirmation: I will reflect daily on the Word of God, which is my spiritual resource against negativity.

My Need for Guidance

I will pray and ask for God's direction in all decisions that I make every day.

This would be a stress-buster if I consulted God before I did a deep dive in whatever I think I should be doing. Discernment is needed, and a conversation with God is needed to obtain discernment. Without my spiritual GPS (global positioning system), I go 100 miles in the wrong direction. However, when I listen to the Holy Spirit, he tells me, "Route, re-route, make a U-turn at the next intersection." What situations have you heard the Holy Spirit command you to re-route?

What was the outcome when you did or didn't obey the command?

Proverbs 3:5–6 says, "Trust in the Lord with all thine heart; And lean not unto thine own understanding. In all thy ways acknowledge him, and he shall direct thy paths." King James Version (KJV)

My Reflections and Meditation:

_____

_____

_____

_____

_____

_____

_____

_____

_____

_____

_____

_____

_____

_____

_____

_____

_____

_____

_____

_____

_____

_____

_____

_____

_____

_____

_____

My Reflections and Meditation:

_____

_____

_____

_____

_____

_____

_____

_____

_____

_____

_____

_____

_____

_____

_____

_____

_____

_____

_____

_____

_____

_____

_____

_____

_____

_____

_____

Affirmation: I will use the many spiritual GPS's available to me: The Word of God, Prayer, Meditation and Resting in Him, etc., before putting into action my mental decisions.

My Purpose

Today I celebrate that because God loves me, I am alive to fulfill his purpose.

At age 7, I knew I wanted to be a nurse. My wonderful mom was mentally ill off and on when I was that age, and I learned compassion and caregiving at an early age. When my father asked me what I wanted to be when I grew up, I confidently said "a nurse." When I was in high school, I joined the Future Nurses' Club and learned basic first aid. It was exciting to me to know that I could relieve suffering by becoming this person called a nurse. My father encouraged me but said, "be a full nurse." He meant go all the way in my education. Now having been in the profession for over 40 years and 24 of those years as a Certified Nurse Practitioner, I serve with joy knowing that with God's grace I have fulfilled my promise to my dad and myself to "go all the way." I have been able to speak with patients and co-workers about life changes with Christ and make my office a sanctuary for myself and others. What does going "all the way" in your purpose look like? Have you begun or are you continuing your life's purpose, despite set-backs?

1 Peter 1:2 says, "You were chosen according to the purpose of God the Father and were made a Holy People by His Spirit, to obey Jesus Christ and be purified by His blood. May Grace and peace be yours in full measure." GNBUK: Good News Bible (Anglicized) 1994

Jeremiah 1:5 "Before I made you in your mother's womb, I chose you. Before you were born, I set you apart for a special work. I appointed you a prophet to the nations." International Children's Bible (ICB)

My Reflections and Meditation:

_____
_____
_____
_____
_____
_____
_____
_____
_____
_____
_____
_____
_____
_____
_____
_____
_____
_____
_____
_____
_____
_____
_____
_____
_____
_____

My Reflections and Meditation:

_____

_____

_____

_____

_____

_____

_____

_____

_____

_____

_____

_____

_____

_____

_____

_____

_____

_____

_____

_____

_____

_____

_____

_____

_____

_____

_____

My Reflections and Meditation:

_____
_____
_____
_____
_____
_____
_____
_____
_____
_____
_____
_____
_____
_____
_____
_____
_____
_____
_____
_____
_____
_____
_____
_____
_____
_____
_____

Affirmation: I will use my daily work as a ministry to the ones God sends my way. My service, God's way.

My Gloomy Outlook

The enemy is a liar; I am not a mistake!

I don't need anyone else to put a dark cloud over my head — I can do that myself. It seems that when goals are not met according to my timeline, or disappointments arrive back-to-back, I get down in the dumps. The bigger the disappointment, the bigger the dump truck. It carries my "stinking thinking" and drags me down the path of discouragement. Then the rain comes and drenches me, wrapping me in a fog of defeatism. But praise be to God, I am beginning to look at the rain as liquid sunshine. After all, it must be sunny somewhere; it just hasn't reached me yet. Like the musical in which Annie says, "...the sun'll come out tomorrow." I serve the God who created the sun and the rain. I can thrive in both seasons. Can you see the silver lining behind the clouds of your situation? Don't you know God allows the sun to shine on the just and the unjust. Rejoice, it is always sunny somewhere: clouds are always moving out of the way!

1 Peter 1:6 says, "In this you greatly rejoice, though now for a little while, if need be, you have been grieved by various trials…." NKJV

My Reflections and Meditation:

_____
_____
_____
_____
_____
_____
_____
_____
_____
_____
_____
_____
_____
_____
_____
_____
_____
_____
_____
_____
_____
_____
_____
_____
_____
_____

My Reflections and Meditation:

_____

_____

_____

_____

_____

_____

_____

_____

_____

_____

_____

_____

_____

_____

_____

_____

_____

_____

_____

_____

_____

_____

_____

_____

_____

Affirmation: I rely on the Word of God that instructs me to walk by faith and not by sight.

My Past

God has forgiven me for my past mistakes and sins, and I must forgive myself so I can move on from the past.

We have a past, present, and future, but how many of us, including me, tend to dwell in the past. If it is joy we are experiencing, that would be great and inspiring — but many times we carry the so-called baggage of despair. We continue to rehearse the *woulda–coulda–shouldas* of the experiences we may or may not have had control over. So, does that help us or hinder us? We have put ourselves on a pedestal (maybe I am talking to myself) and we do fail in that aspect. We fail to remember that we are imperfect sinful beings who are only redeemed by Christ. Yet He loves us despite our failings (sins) and always gives us another chance for improvement. So that is reason to rejoice and look forward instead of backward and pitch the baggage of the past, so we won't have excess weight on our journey! The enemy of God and man wants to defeat us through our minds, so what painful experiences can you pitch in the dumpster, wash your hands, (and your thoughts) and grab God's and move on!

Micah 7:19 says, "He will again have compassion on us; He will tread our iniquities [sins] underfoot. You will cast all our sins into the depths of the sea." (ESV)

My Reflections and Meditation:

My Reflections and Meditation:

_____

_____

_____

_____

_____

_____

_____

_____

_____

_____

_____

_____

_____

_____

_____

_____

_____

_____

_____

_____

_____

_____

_____

My Reflections and Meditation:

Affirmation: I will realize that the past is a part of my human history, but unless it is positive there is no need for it in my future, except to learn from it and strive not to repeat it.

My Future

It doesn't matter what my present situation looks like, I am growing in God's Grace and Mercy, and in Christ I will be victorious.

Philippians 4:13 says, "I can do all things through Christ who strengthens me." NKJV

It seems like the older I get, the closer the future is. Meaning I begin to have concern about having enough time to achieve what I feel is my God-given calling. I have mentored younger people and I caution them on not wasting their gifts, nor spending unmeaningful time while enjoying their youth. Situations can put the brakes on what we want to achieve, so in order to keep the momentum we need to keep pressing forward. Challenging times may cause us to change course, and that is all right as long as we continue to ask for guidance in partnerships, career choices, and finances. Our future does not have to resemble another's since we are all gifted differently. The matter is to know that there is a Holy force behind us, pushing us to our destined future. Is there something holding you back from your goals? Is it someone or something else, or is it just you?

My Reflections and Meditation:

_____

_____

_____

_____

_____

_____

_____

_____

_____

_____

_____

_____

_____

_____

_____

_____

_____

_____

_____

_____

_____

_____

_____

_____

My Reflections and Meditation:

_____

_____

_____

_____

_____

_____

_____

_____

_____

_____

_____

_____

_____

_____

_____

_____

_____

_____

_____

_____

_____

_____

_____

_____

_____

_____

_____

Affirmation: I look forward to a future of possibilities despite my current situations and despite my age.

My Emotions

I will not let anxiety or depression keep me from having the life God has planned for me.

Self-sabotaging — wow, I am good at this. I recently learned of a concept called "the Imposter Syndrome." Well, I didn't like this term, because I didn't want to think it applied to me. After all, I didn't want to think that I was pretending to be something I am not; I am not a phony! Then I read the definition, which was the opposite of what I thought it meant: "The persistent inability to believe that one's success is deserved, or has been legitimately achieved as a result of one's own efforts or skills." Oh my, I can think of so many times I missed opportunities because I didn't think I was knowledgeable enough to fulfill a particular request. The definition goes on to say, "People suffering from Imposter Syndrome may be at increased risk of anxiety." So, I examine my emotions and see if this is a temporary state of mind, or if I am troubled continually. Do I need professional help to explore the reasons behind this behavior? Have you missed opportunities because of self-sabotage?

Jeremiah 29:11 says, "'For I know the plans and thoughts that I have for you,' says the Lord, 'plans for peace and wellbeing and not for disaster, to give you a future and a hope.'" Amplified Bible (AMP)

My Reflections and Meditation:

_____

_____

_____

_____

_____

_____

_____

_____

_____

_____

_____

_____

_____

_____

_____

_____

_____

_____

_____

_____

_____

_____

_____

_____

_____

_____

_____

My Reflections and Meditation:

_____
_____
_____
_____
_____
_____
_____
_____
_____
_____
_____
_____
_____
_____
_____
_____
_____
_____
_____
_____
_____
_____
_____
_____
_____
_____
_____
_____

Affirmation: Since God had plans for my purpose before I was born, I put aside anxiety and depressed feelings so I can fulfill my purpose. I will seek a professional evaluation if having chronic emotional distress.

My Power

I turn my back and walk or run away from the enemy; he has no power over me.

This present age is being bombarded by the evil one, the prince of the air. He is wreaking havoc on the world knowing his time is coming to a close. Hallelujah! Sickness, death, lies, and injustices are all a part of his tactics to overcome good with evil. So how do we dispel darkness? In the physical realm, we light a candle, we turn on a light switch, the sun comes up, and darkness is dispelled. In the spiritual realm, we carry the Light within us, which is God's Holy Spirit. He is our helper, companion, and interprets our moaning's when we cannot pray. We are overcomers because Jesus Christ overcame the darkness of the world. He did not leave us alone when He physically left; the Holy Spirit is His gift to us. How and where can you use your God-given power to shed light in dark spiritual places?

James 4:7 says, "Submit yourselves, then, to God. Resist the devil, and he will flee from you." NIV

My Reflections and Meditation:

_____
_____
_____
_____
_____
_____
_____
_____
_____
_____
_____
_____
_____
_____
_____
_____
_____
_____
_____
_____
_____
_____
_____
_____
_____

My Reflections and Meditation:

_____

_____

_____

_____

_____

_____

_____

_____

_____

_____

_____

_____

_____

_____

_____

_____

_____

_____

_____

_____

_____

_____

_____

_____

_____

_____

_____

_____

_____

Affirmation: I have the Power of God within me. He provides an escape route for me. I am able to overcome evil through His strength.

My Unforgiving Spirit

What has hurt me, cannot hinder me. I look at the pain of the past and consider the word "Past."

Previous, yet painful circumstances have helped me grow into the person I am. It is just a piece of the puzzle of life. I can release that burden to God and allow Him to heal me. There is no future in unforgiveness; my future has been established by Him who created me. I need to think about whom I need to forgive, even if the person is me. Why am I letting this hold me back? What daily steps can I take to move forward? Unforgiveness should not put a heavy weight on me and keep me from getting where God wants me to be. Since I am forgiven by God, I must also forgive. I thank God for dismissing the negative messages that I carry in my mind. Are you carrying the burden of unforgiveness? Doesn't it feel heavy and crowd your mind so you can't focus on what God has for you? Can you release the person by forgiving them? Or do you want to remain shackled to the incident of the past and be a prisoner of your own making?

Jeremiah 29:11–13 says, "For I know the thoughts that I think toward you, says the Lord, thoughts of peace and not of evil, to give you a future and a hope. Then you will call upon Me and go and pray to Me, and I will listen to you. And you will seek Me and find Me, when you search for Me with all your heart." NKJV

Matthew 6:12 ."and forgive us our debts, as we forgive our debtors (letting go of both the wrong and the resentment). Amplified

My Reflections and Meditation:

_____
_____
_____
_____
_____
_____
_____
_____
_____
_____
_____
_____
_____
_____
_____
_____
_____
_____
_____
_____
_____
_____
_____
_____
_____
_____

My Reflections and Meditation:

My Reflections and Meditation:

_____
_____
_____
_____
_____
_____
_____
_____
_____
_____
_____
_____
_____
_____
_____
_____
_____
_____
_____
_____
_____
_____
_____
_____
_____
_____
_____

Affirmation: I am ready for freedom and I am released from bondage and choose to forgive.

My Anticipation

My community, country, and the world are waiting for my God-given gifts to be released; there is no one else like me.

As I overcome shyness and lack of confidence and strive to empower myself, I can encourage others to do the same. I have untapped skills to use, and have more to learn to fulfill my purpose and express God's glory. God has not given us a spirit of fear, but of power, love, and a sound mind.

He says if anyone lacks wisdom to ask Him and He gives freely. What have you been afraid to pursue? Have you talked to your father God about it? If not, will you ask Him for a date, and meet with Him to discuss it. He is a Divine loving partner!

Philippians 3:14 says, "I press toward the goal for the prize of the upward call of God in Christ Jesus." NKJV

My Reflections and Meditation:

_____
_____
_____
_____
_____
_____
_____
_____
_____
_____
_____
_____
_____
_____
_____
_____
_____
_____
_____
_____
_____
_____
_____
_____

My Reflections and Meditation:

_____
_____
_____
_____
_____
_____
_____
_____
_____
_____
_____
_____
_____
_____
_____
_____
_____
_____
_____
_____
_____
_____
_____

Affirmation: I have been appointed good works for such a time as this.

My Difficulties

As Fannie Lou Hamer said, "I'm sick and tired of being sick and tired."

Most times I try to be grateful, but then get into the pity party business, and keep passing out invitations, repeating the slogan "why me?" It seems like trouble comes in bunches and that I take three steps forward and then five steps back. My get up and go has gotten up and went — so to speak.

As I go through this life, I acknowledge that there will be difficult days, weeks, or maybe months to years. I am grateful for challenges as well as successes. Each day I wake up, I know that God has kept me through His Grace and Mercy. I am assured that He who is in me is greater than he who is in the world. In John 16:33, Jesus says, "These things I have spoken to you, that in Me you may have peace. In the world you will have tribulation; but be of good cheer, I have overcome the world." (NKJV)

What unexpected difficulties have arisen in your life recently? Are you in a storm, coming out of a storm, or going into a storm? Consult with God. Not only is He a Storm Chaser, but He is the Storm Squelcher!

My Reflections and Meditation:

My Reflections and Meditation:

_____

_____

_____

_____

_____

_____

_____

_____

_____

_____

_____

_____

_____

_____

_____

_____

_____

_____

_____

_____

_____

_____

_____

Affirmation: God gives me the strength and resources to meet each day with confidence.

My Joy

If happiness escapes me (which is short term), I will choose joy (which is long term).

These are concepts that were hard for me to understand initially. After all, if I am happy, doesn't that mean I have joy? Well, no. An easy interpretation I have heard is that happiness is based on happenings or external situations. In other words, if everything is going well in your life and surroundings, you will feel good about it — as long as the situation doesn't change. This is based on present circumstances.

However, joy is based on internal feelings. Gratitude and peace can give you that feeling. Referring to Compassion.com, the site for Compassion International, I found great comparisons between Happiness and Joy. One of them states, "Joy is in the heart. Happiness is on the face." Another states, "Joy transcends. Happiness reacts." So, I may see that someone is happy, but may not see the joy. This is especially true when there is suffering or misfortune.

So, do I express happiness only? Despite my circumstances can I express joy — which is a Fruit of the Spirit?

My Reflections and Meditation:

_____
_____
_____
_____
_____
_____
_____
_____
_____
_____
_____
_____
_____
_____
_____
_____
_____
_____
_____
_____
_____
_____
_____
_____
_____
_____

My Reflections and Meditation:

_____
_____
_____
_____
_____
_____
_____
_____
_____
_____
_____
_____
_____
_____
_____
_____
_____
_____
_____
_____
_____
_____
_____
_____
_____

Affirmation: When happiness is nowhere to be found, I rely on the fact that Jesus is the center of my Joy (line from song "Center of My Joy," by Richard Smallwood). I choose Joy because it is His gift to me.

Psalm 5:11 says, "But let all those rejoice who put their trust in You; Let them ever shout for joy, because you defend them; Let those also who Love your name Be joyful in You." NKJV

My Relationships

My connections to others can lead to positive or negative outcomes.

God has created me to glorify Him with my life. He has also created us to be in community; however, there are people and situations that affect how I react. I need to be mindful that I have no control over anyone except myself. On challenging days, that may be difficult as well. I want to be able to display the character of Jesus, so that others see Him in my actions, rather than just seeing me. I pray that the depressed will feel compassion, the angry will feel understood, and the lonely will feel a sense of community. What do others sense when I am around them? Does my participation in gossip and negativity turn others away from Christ? Or do I create an atmosphere of love and warmth that can draw the hurting toward Him? What impact could I have if my life expressed the Fruit of the Spirit?

My Reflections and Meditation:

_____
_____
_____
_____
_____
_____
_____
_____
_____
_____
_____
_____
_____
_____
_____
_____
_____
_____
_____
_____
_____
_____
_____
_____
_____
_____
_____
_____
_____

My Reflections and Meditation:

_____
_____
_____
_____
_____
_____
_____
_____
_____
_____
_____
_____
_____
_____
_____
_____
_____
_____
_____
_____
_____
_____
_____
_____
_____
_____

Affirmation: I will hold on to relationships that nurture my relationship with Jesus Christ, and I will let go of negative hurtful relationships that causes anger, depressing or anxious feelings toward others or myself.

Galatians 5:22–23 says, "But the fruit of the Spirit is love, joy, peace, patience, kindness, goodness, faithfulness, gentleness, and self-control. The law is not against such things." Christian Standard Bible (CSB)

My Love Life

As I embody the characteristics of Christ, and if it is His will for me to have a mate, He will send the one He has created for me to complement my personality and Christ-like values.

Secular (worldly) life gives us all types of messages of what love is, how you get love, how you keep it and what you will feel like when you lose it. This has been hyped up due to social media, where we are bombarded by what attracts the opposite sex, and generally "sex" is the operative word. Physical characteristics are emphasized. In other words, what you see is what you get. So many young people — and especially females — are encouraged to compare themselves to others. With poor self-esteem, they are duped into behaving in ways that put their God created bodies on display in efforts to attract what they think is "love." We see that recently on social media. Like a store mannequin, they can be dressed up or down depending on the situation. Secular songs have great dance beats, but how many actually listen to the lyrics closely? Subliminal (unconscious) messages are there. For the most part, they are demeaning to women and also give men the liberty to call women degrading names. Women may also be pulled into the notion of what society thinks are acceptable male characteristics, for example his looks, physique, cash flow, status in the community, etc. All of these are stamped "temporary" and without any spiritual or moral compass those physical attributes are declining investments. Rather than rushing into unstable relationships, can we wait for God to reward us with the One especially created for us? "Till death do us part" may be a very long time.

Proverbs 31:10–12 says, "Who can find a virtuous wife? For her worth *is* far above rubies. The heart of her husband safely trusts her; So he will have no lack of gain. She does him good and not evil All the days of her life." NKJV

My Reflections and Meditation:

My Reflections and Meditation:

My Reflections and Meditation:

_____

_____

_____

_____

_____

_____

_____

_____

_____

_____

_____

_____

_____

_____

_____

_____

_____

_____

_____

_____

_____

_____

_____

_____

_____

Affirmation: I will consider my behaviors in trying to attract a mate. I know God does all things well. He is maturing me and my future mate to give Him glory first, then creates us as gifts to each other in His time.

Proverbs 18:22 says, "*He who* finds a wife finds a good thing, And finds favor from the Lord." NKJV

My Home Life

The size of the home does not matter, but the family residing in the home does; I will consider the characteristics of my home.

You may have been in a biological family, an extended one, an adopted family, or a step-family; all of these types will have some effect on your adulthood. My family of origin was small. My father was an only child and I have only one sibling, a younger sister, since my brother died a few days after birth. Both of my parents were from South Carolina. My father raised us in a private, strict home with emphasis on education and church. My mother, who became mentally ill when I was 7 years old, came from a large family, and she was used to big family gatherings and hard work on the farm. Who I am was shaped by these contrasts. My own home life through re-marriage, has had challenges, but we serve a God who is able to help us overcome them. Transparency is freeing. God has been working on us and restoring us. Thanks be to God.

In reflecting on the life of Jesus, being the Son of God and not conceived with human conception, I know he had a step-father Joseph, his mother Mary's future husband. He later had siblings who were his step-brothers and sisters, who followed Jesus' ministry. After the crucifixion of Jesus, his step-brothers James and Jude carried his messages in the Bible. Such love was not born out of easy times I am sure, but somehow reflected their home life. What does your home life reflect? What do the family members who live there say about their home? Can you share with God how you would like to have a home reflecting Him?

My Reflections and Meditation:

_____

_____

_____

_____

_____

_____

_____

_____

_____

_____

_____

_____

_____

_____

_____

_____

_____

_____

_____

_____

_____

_____

_____

_____

_____

_____

My Reflections and Meditation:

My Reflections and Meditation:

_____

_____

_____

_____

_____

_____

_____

_____

_____

_____

_____

_____

_____

_____

_____

_____

_____

_____

_____

_____

_____

_____

_____

_____

_____

Affirmation: I will strive to take the positives I received at home and carry them through my life, and I will seek help if needed, to prevent the negatives from being repeated.

Psalm 101:2 says, "I will be careful to live a blameless life — when will you come to help me? I will lead a life of integrity in my own home." New Living Translation (NLT)

My Homeless State

When I was homeless, the Lord provided a home.

Home is where the heart is, it has been said, and I can relate to that. When my parents separated, my mom took my sister and me to another state, and we were taken in by my aunt and uncle and their children (our cousins). They treated us as if we belonged there without any grumbling or making us feel unwanted. We were assigned chores like our cousins, and my aunt helped my mother get us enrolled in school there, and never at one time did I realize I was homeless, because I was in a loving home. So as a health care professional now, I care for many underserved citizens, many of whom are homeless. It breaks my heart to see fellow human beings sleeping in tents on the streets and under viaducts; however, many of them consider that their home. Have you observed the homeless? They still have a sense of community. Consider the many reasons for someone being homeless and with compassion, help when you can.

My Reflections and Meditation:

My Reflections and Meditation:

_____
_____
_____
_____
_____
_____
_____
_____
_____
_____
_____
_____
_____
_____
_____
_____
_____
_____
_____
_____
_____
_____
_____
_____

Affirmation: I will consider what it is like to be homeless, and have empathy for my fellow sisters and brothers who are. If I have the means to be a change maker, I will put forth that effort.

Romans 12:16 says, "Be of the same mind toward one another. Do not set your mind on high things, but associate with the humble. Do not be wise in your own opinion." NKJV

My Career

I see my job as a ministry to others instead of just a means to make money.

Most of us who work outside of the home spend more time there than we do at home with family. As believers in Christ, we are on a platform to display his love and power since those around us are watching to see if "we walk the walk and not just talk the talk." So how do we show His love in our time at work? The prayer of St. Francis of Assisi states, "Not so much seek to…be understood as to understand." How we respond to bickering and fatigue, being short staffed and others taking longer than approved breaks, can be annoying and discouraging. In reflecting on how Jesus handled misjustices, he didn't shy away from them but addressed them head on. Like the man who had buried his Talent because he only had one. It was taken away and given to the one who had more but continued to use it as required. Or the man who worked the field more hours than the one who got to work later, but they both were paid the same. The one who worked more hours was angry. Jesus let him know that the Master of the field could do as he pleased with his money. Many times, we are unhappy at work because we are jealous of someone, or idolize ourselves on the job. This is misery, not ministry.

Those of us in leadership positions may want to reflect on Sir Richard Branson's quote: "Train them so they can leave. Treat them well enough so they don't want to." Are you a servant leader? Or could you be a servant follower?

My Reflections and Meditation:

_____
_____
_____
_____
_____
_____
_____
_____
_____
_____
_____
_____
_____
_____
_____
_____
_____
_____
_____
_____
_____
_____
_____
_____

My Reflections and Meditation:

My Reflections and Meditation:

_____
_____
_____
_____
_____
_____
_____
_____
_____
_____
_____
_____
_____
_____
_____
_____
_____
_____
_____
_____
_____
_____
_____
_____
_____
_____

Affirmation: I will see my work as a service to others, and lead by example so others can see Christ. He has the ultimate judgment of what reward each should be given.

Acts 20:35 says, "I have shown you in every way, by laboring like this, that you must support the weak. And remember the words of the Lord Jesus, that He said, "It is more blessed to give than to receive." NKJV

My Mood Booster — Laughter

Today I will look for situations that can make me laugh. However, not situations that ridicule others.

Laughter is healthy. It makes one breathe deeper, boosts the brain endorphins — the feel-good chemicals — and it is one method to decrease cortisol levels, the stress hormone. High and sustained levels of cortisol lead to many diseases. Many people use drugs or alcohol to boost their moods, but studies have shown that behavior worsens the mood overtime and increases drug or alcohol dependency. We don't want that! If you can't surround yourself with happy people, or if you have daily stressors in life or on your job, then read a comic strip, or a book with healthy jokes, or go to a funny movie. See how your outlook is for the rest of the day, and how your changed outlook can impact others as well. Being a "Debbie or Dennis Downer" either pushes people away from you or attracts more people who are negative. What mood boosters can you provide to your environment? Or do you just "bring on the noise"?

My Reflections and Meditation:

My Reflections and Meditation:

_____

_____

_____

_____

_____

_____

_____

_____

_____

_____

_____

_____

_____

_____

_____

_____

_____

_____

_____

_____

_____

_____

_____

_____

_____

Affirmation: I am able to find humor daily and spread joy with others.

Proverbs 15:13 says, "A cheerful heart brings a smile to your face; a sad heart makes it hard to get through the day." The Message Bible (MSG)

My Health

I will grow through the different stages of my life and be a reflection of Jesus for others to see.

I have several chronic conditions, some of which may be genetic, meaning it runs in my family genes. Most days I feel great. This requires me to take medication, watch my diet, increase exercise in order to keep a healthy weight and not further cause damage to my vital organs. Due to my own conditions, I am able to share this information with others. Hopefully this will give them information to improve their health as well. There is also my emotional and spiritual health. Neglecting those needs will not give me a totally healthy life. If I need to speak with a counselor or have pastoral guidance, it provides holistic care. Knowing I have fewer years ahead of me, I have already prepared advanced directives, a draft of my funeral, and my will, which will be finalized by a lawyer. This is to provide some guidance for my family in preparing for my death and to leave whatever I can for their use. Doing that can be considered a final gift. The family stress of trying to figure that out is unnecessary. Have you considered your last days and what preparation you can make to ease the psychological and financial burdens on those left behind? When will you prepare a will and funeral arrangements for your Home going?

My Reflections and Meditation:

_____

_____

_____

_____

_____

_____

_____

_____

_____

_____

_____

_____

_____

_____

_____

_____

_____

_____

_____

_____

_____

_____

_____

_____

_____

_____

_____

_____

My Reflections and Meditation:

_____
_____
_____
_____
_____
_____
_____
_____
_____
_____
_____
_____
_____
_____
_____
_____
_____
_____
_____
_____
_____
_____
_____
_____
_____
_____
_____

Affirmation: I will seek guidance in caring for my health but will prepare for the end of my life as well.

Deuteronomy 30:19–20 says, "Today I ask heaven and earth to be witnesses. I am offering you life or death, blessings or curses. Now, choose life! Then you and your children may live. To choose life is to love the Lord your God, obey Him and stay close to Him.…" New Century Version (NCV)

My Prayer Life

Every day I will make time to spend time with God in thankfulness, not in just making requests.

So, we know that prayer is simply communication. Talking with God. Many times, I know I may be speaking in gibberish. Overwhelmed at times at asking for too much of God and not starting with being thankful. Suppose our children kept asking for stuff, not thinking about what we have already given them. Suppose they did not say, "thank you, or I appreciate you, or you have blessed my life, Mom or Dad." How would we feel. Disappointed? Neglected? Angry? After all, children usually don't know the sacrifices that were made to get them what they need or where they need to go. God sacrificed His only begotten Son so that our sins would be forgiven, and we can be given the pathway to Eternal Life. When I think about it — no more sickness, death, strife, poverty — that is more than enough to say thank you when God in His grace and mercy gives me another day! Does your prayer begin with telling our creator "*thank you*"? He is a generous father and worthy of all our praise!

My Reflections and Meditation:

_____
_____
_____
_____
_____
_____
_____
_____
_____
_____
_____
_____
_____
_____
_____
_____
_____
_____
_____
_____
_____
_____
_____
_____
_____
_____

My Reflections and Meditation:

_____

_____

_____

_____

_____

_____

_____

_____

_____

_____

_____

_____

_____

_____

_____

_____

_____

_____

_____

_____

_____

_____

_____

_____

_____

_____

_____

Affirmation: My time is God's Time; I will set aside time each day to be in His presence with Thankful Prayer.

Matthew 6:9–11 "In this manner, therefore, pray: Our Father in heaven, Hallowed be Your name. Your kingdom come. Your will be done on earth as *it is* in heaven. Give us this day our daily bread." NKJV

Now Dear One — pray, listen for God's voice, and write your own special meditation for your journey. Where are you now physically, emotionally, or spiritually? What is God telling you about your purpose?

Philippians 1:6 says, "...being confident of this very thing, that He who has begun a good work in you will complete *it* until the day of Jesus Christ" NKJV

My Reflections and Meditation:

About the Author

Vivianne A. Griffiths, M.S.N., A.P.R.N., was born and grew up in Brooklyn, New York. She has lived in three other states and has lived in Louisville, Kentucky, for more than 30 years with her husband, George. They have two adult children — son, Abayomi Browne, and daughter, Dionne Griffiths.

Vivianne is a retired Adult Nurse Practitioner, whose last employment was with a Federally Qualified Health Center in the West End of Louisville, providing medical care for a diverse population across gender and ethnic backgrounds. She has precepted many nurse practitioner students from local colleges of nursing and selected as one of the 2021 Health Care Heroes by Louisville Business First.

In 2013, she became a Certified Christian Life Coach through the Christian Coach Institute with Janice LaVore-Fletcher and went on to obtain certifications for Teen Girls Life Coach through Teen Wisdom Life Coach program, with Tammi Walsh — 2017; and Personal Development Life Coach through the CaPP Institute, with Valorie Burton — 2020

She is an active member of Canaan Christian Church, under the leadership of Dr. Walter Malone, Jr., founder and pastor.

Vivianne is the founder and CEO of Arise and Go Forth, LLC Life Coaching for Teen Girls and Women

Vivianne can be contacted at www.ariseandgoforth.com